AUTHORS NOTE

King Solomon the wisest of all men wrote in the book of Mishlei that the strength and splendor of a woman are her clothing...Charm is false and beauty is futile. A woman who fears God should be praised...

This booklet can help young couples, women at all ages and men to understand the wisdom behind the song Eshet Chayil - A Woman of Valour.

This booklet will unravel the secret ingredient to live a life with modesty.

You will find interesting ideas and thoughts for everyone on how to utilize the power of modesty to illuminate and transform your life.

This booklet will show you how you can bring holiness into your home, how to bring good health into your home and enrich your lives in every way just by dressing modestly.

The stories in this booklet emphasize the deeper concepts of modesty with clarity, showing its beauty and reward. It raises the woman to a new level, a level of bringing the Shechinah, the presence of HaShem into her home. What a precious gift to uphold for eternity! For all future generations to follow...

ACKNOWLEDGEMENT

With immense gratitude to HaShem for the merit
He granted me to complete this booklet and for the
endless miracles and protection HaShem performed
to me personally and our family.

One of the most acute problems in our generation is
a lack of clarity and understanding of the concept of
modesty.

There is a need to distinguish between the normal
and the abnormal in life. In our days the normal is
viewed as being abnormal and the abnormal is
viewed as normal. Walking down the street we can
clearly see many women dressed very immodestly
who truly think that they are modest and that it is
completely normal to look this way.

The ultimate purpose of this book is to guide and
encourage women to improve their spiritual lives,
gradually achieving perfection in modesty. Modesty
draws us closer to our Creator. It teaches us how to
climb the ladder step by step to achieve our goal.

With God's Help this booklet will benefit many
women who seek to know the secrets of Modesty.
With HaShem's Kindness may every chapter of this
book bring you closer to perform the Mitzvah of
modesty.

DEDICATION

I dedicate this book in honor of my dear and precious husband Tzvi Harbor. I love you very much and can never thank you enough for all you do for us. Anything that I have accomplished has come about only because of your encouragement, advice, and guidance. May HaShem keep you healthy and strong always to 120.

In the merit of this booklet may HaShem grant Tzvi ben Malka Molly perfect health, may he continue to grow in Torah learning, may we merit much Jewish Nachat from all of our children and grandchildren...

As our children have Baruch HaShem grown and have their own families we ask HaShem to watch over them, keep them healthy and strong, keep them growing in Torah and Mitzvot and merit to continue to live in the land of Israel forever in good health and wisdom of the Torah.

Toda Raba to my precious son Shlomo for helping me with this booklet. His wise counsel, time and knowledge of the computer allowed me to complete this booklet. May HaShem grant him good health, growth in Torah learning, and may he merit to build a Bayit NeEman BeYsrael.

Dedicated in loving memory of our dear parents and grandparents.

Imi moraty Beila Sora bat Chaim and Sheina ז"ל

Avi mori Yechezkel ben Alter and Leah ז"ל

Malka Molly bat Zeev and Elsa ז"ל

Aharon ben Tzvi Harris ben Frida ז"ל

Avraham Yitzchak ben Sender ז"ל

Sheina bat Avraham and Leah ז"ל

Chaim ben Mendel laib and Reizel ז"ל

Pessach ben Chaim and Sheina ז"ל

My dear aunt Belha Bat Moshe and Sara ז"ל

 My father's sister who was killed during the
holocaust- Beila Sora bat Alter and Leah ז"ל

My father's brother Sender ben Alter and Leah ז"ל
who was killed in the Russian army during the
holocaust for being Jewish.

Moshe Leib ben Alter and Leah ז"ל - my father's
brother who was killed during the holocaust.

Our dear friend Zack Liner Zelig ben Motel.

May they be good intermediary for us and Klal
Israel and may their Neshama have an elevation.

Toda Raba to my dear friend Galit Zer Chen. You were always so generous with your time and advice.

You are a busy wife, mother, lecturer and a Rabbanit. You were so kind to give me endless hours of your time. You enhanced this booklet by telling me new stories to enhance the understanding and importance of the Mitzvah of Modesty to the readers of this booklet.

Your input, advice and experience were of immeasurable help. You enveloped me with inspiration and encouragement to complete and publish this booklet.

As we get closer to completing this work after so many years, I extend my heartfelt gratitude to my precious friend Menucha Rochel who spent hours of her time to edit this booklet. Without her encouragement and her input this booklet would not have been published.

Your friendship Menucha Rochel is truly a gift from HaShem. Thank you so much for giving me the opportunity to do something meaningful for every woman who would like to understand the most profound matter of modestly.

This booklet is showing us how to prepare ourselves to enter the new millennium with modesty and dignity. Thank you Menucha Rochel for helping me to reveal the hidden secret of modesty…

Some of the articles in this book are from many sources and are combined together....

May HaKadosh Baruch Hu Bless Galit and her entire family and Menucha Rochel and her entire family with Nachat, Mazal and perfect health, much strength to continue their important work each in her own interest. Thanks for being there for me and for your loving kindness.

Shoshana Harbor

Remember our wedding day? The world stood still as I descended to heaven and chose you to be My beloved.

With Mt. Sinai as our chuppah and the Torah our ketubah, it was the happiest day of my life.

I admit, we've had our rough patches, but who else do you know whose marriage has lasted for over three thousand years.

I've been thinking. Lets renew our vows. We begin the Holiday of Shavuot, celebrating the anniversary of God giving us the Torah at Mount Sinai, the revelation at Sinai. Every year on this holiday God reaffirms His covenant with the Jewish people, just as we reaffirm our relationship with HaShem by accepting the Torah once again…

Shavuot is the day that we and God celebrate our anniversary, God says to the Jewish people "Because of the special love I have for you, I would like to share a hidden secret I have stored in my possession, go and share it with my beloved daughters; go and let them know the extraordinary reward that awaits them for being my modest daughters."

Please remember My commandments and be a modest woman, please follow in the footsteps of your foremothers. Please remember to reward HaShem with the gift of modesty. Unlike all gifts this one is reserved only for my royal daughters. I invite all of you to come and celebrate the completion of this booklet *The Hidden Secrets of Modesty* with me...

Avraham is a student of Torah who greets everyone with a friendly smile and a warm hello. One day he was returning home from his Yeshiva hungry and tired. On the way home he found himself standing near an apple tree. He ate an apple and then another and another until he fell asleep.

When he awoke the next morning he realized that he ate from a tree which didn't belong to him. According to the Code of Jewish Law the apples which were taken without permission from the neighbors yard render them to be stolen.

Avraham being a very honest young man wanted to ask HaShem for forgiveness. He decided to go to the neighbor. He knocked at his door explaining how tired he was and how he found himself near the tree eating the apples. The young man who opened the door agreed to forgive him under the condition that he marries his sister. Avraham agreed to that spontaneous and unpredictable deal. Even though the brother had pointed out that his sister can't see, he agreed to marry her.

You must go to my brother who lives across from me, he too is the owner of the tree, so Avraham the righteous young man that he was did just that, he knocked on the second brothers door. A young man opened it. Repeating the story again the second brother promised to forgive him under the condition he marries his sister. He agreed even though the brother had told him that his sister can't walk.

You must go to my brother who lives upstairs, he is the owner of the tree and ask for an apology. When the third brother opened the door he promised to forgive him if he marries his sister. Avraham agreed although he was told she didn't speak.

He was asked to apologize to the fourth brother, after all he is the owner of the tree too. He knocks on the fourth brothers door and sure enough the deal was the same. If you are willing to marry my sister I will forgive you. He then turned to the fourth brother and told him that he will marry his sister, even though she can't see, hear, and walk... She can't talk either said the brother.

I will marry her under the condition that she will be well covered during the wedding so I won't be able to see her.

The wedding was very glamorous although the bride and the groom didn't see each other.

After the wedding Avraham was sitting on the sofa sad and heartbroken asking HaShem why he deserved such a wife who can't see, speak, hear and walk...When suddenly he hears a sweet and gentle voice asking him - would you like me to make you a cup of tea?...

He turns to see where this voice is coming from, and seeing the young woman in front of him he asked, who are you? It is me your wife, she answered, he looked at her and saw a beautiful woman who can walk, hear, talk and see.

Avraham was confused and immediately ran to the brothers to ask them why they all lied to him. The brothers pointed out to Avraham that they didn't lie to him.

By his admission the brothers realized that Avraham is a righteous young man who is deserving of their righteous sister who doesn't walk to inappropriate and immodest places, she doesn't listen to gossip, she doesn't speak evil talk about others and she doesn't look at immodest things. She is a modest young woman and you merted to marry her.

UNCOVERING THE SECRETS OF MODESTY

"Anyone who studies Jewish Law every day can rest assured that he has earned a place in the Next World..." (Talmud Megilla 28b, Niddah 73a) "One who learns in order to teach will be given the ability to learn and to teach but one who learns in order to perform will be given the ability to learn, to teach, to observe and to perform." Avot 4:5

MASTER OF THE UNIVERSE

Please, merciful and benevolent One, help me merit to be a Jewish daughter, righteous and modest.

Remove all the things that deter me from serving You.

Please, HaShem, You are the Helper of all who come to purify themselves.

And you have said, "Open for me an opening the size of a needle and I will open for you an opening the size of a ballroom."

And now, I open for You Father in Heaven an opening like the opening of a needle and I plead before You. "Please HaShem, I want to return to you in complete repentance and to walk with modesty, however, it is difficult for me, I have so many challenges and deterrents.

For You, nothing is difficult. Help me, to overcome with joy all challenges and quickly remove all deterrents.

And I shall merit being a righteous Jewish woman like You desire, who is very happy and delighted to uphold the holy Torah!

And may it be the desire before You that others shall not stumble because of me.

Please HaShem! Merciful and benevolent One, have mercy on me and help me and listen to my prayer because You are the One who listens to prayer.

Blessed is the One who listens to prayers.

WHY DID I START TO COVER MY HAIR?

Head covering became an important and significant part of my life as I discovered its hidden blessings and beauty.

One winter day while waiting to pick up the children from school, I attended a Torah class. Rabbi Parness was an interesting teacher which motivated me to come regularly to the only Orthodox Synagogue in Dayton, Ohio to learn the weekly Torah portion.

One day the Rabbi approached me after class with an unusual question - would you be willing to keep one Shabbat every two months? I was thinking about his unusual request the entire day. By the time my husband finally arrived I had already made up my mind to keep Shabbat every single week. It was the beginning of my spiritual journey.

I often thought about the woman who asked Rabbi Amnon Yitzchak the question of why she couldn't bring a child into this world. Rabbi suggested that she should cover her hair. She hesitated at first and then Rabbi continued by asking her who would she rather see in her home the neighbor or the presence of HaShem?

In Hebrew the two words are very similar, Shchena (neighbor) or the Shechinah (the presence of HaShem). She said the Shechinah, so he said don't worry about the Shchena (the neighbor). She thought for a moment and then decided to cover her hair. She covered her hair and in return HaShem blessed her with a child.

I watched in wonder how what seems to be so minor, impacted her life in such a major way.

I too wanted to be a partner with HaShem in this mighty mitzvah so at first I covered my hair with a wig. When Rabbi Arush requested that I burn my wig and exchange it with a scarf, only at that moment did I begin to understand that the only way to keep this important mitzvah is by simply covering my head with a scarf or a hat.

I feel so blessed to have HaShem's crown on top of my head all day long. As long as the crown is on my head I merit to make a mitzvah every second of my life.

THE DEFINITION OF MODESTY

When we say the word modest we tie it to the way we look outwardly, but modesty begins from within, the way we behave, speak, and react. The modesty of our daughters depends on their gentle, modest, reserved and restrained behavior. To be hidden, not to be noticeable.

Our foremother Sarah, was always in the tent, only when she converted the women was she outside her tent. The Angels wanted to compliment Sarah on her modesty by asking Avraham "where is your wife?" that question increased Avraham's loving feeling toward Sarah.

Sarah Schenirer established Beit Yaakov School for girls in Krakow, Poland. At the completion of this great project, Sages, famous Rabbis and a large crowd gathered to be part of the celebration. Where was Sarah? The one who initiated, built and established the school - where was she? Sarah stood behind with all the other women. This entire mighty project of building this school was built only in her merit. Thanks to her vision of providing our assimilating daughters a Jewish education, the school was built. She knew that those girls are part of one soul determined to grow in Torah and Mitzvot.

She knew that the garden that she had created will continue to produce a glorious assortment of flowers and trees. She knew that each girl will be firmly attached to its roots. She knew that in time those young women would flourish and grow into different trees, flowers and fruits, and rainbows of glorious shades and then hues would appear.

She knew that in time each shoot will be rooted in the same soil, which is the school she so lovingly built, and one day it will stretch its branches and blossom heavenward in an endless pursuit of growth and connection to the One above. Even in this historical moment Sarah Schenirer could have been the most noticeable person there, yet she chose to be hidden and modest.

The Torah praises the modesty of a woman. The Torah shows the woman's worth and her real value through her modesty and proves that she is truly a daughter of Israel - a true daughter of HaShem. The respect and honor of a King's Daughter are all inside and covered.

We don't realize the great power of head covering. However, I would like to share with you the hidden secrets that lie beneath this most mighty mitzvah. Rabbi Chizkiyah (Zohar) said that a woman who covers her hair brings holiness, blessings, peace and prosperity into her home, that her children will become Torah scholars, that her husband will be healthy, and the presence of HaShem will reside in their home.

"Your wife will be like a fruitful vine in the inner recesses of your house (psalm 128:3) your children will be like young olive trees around your table." Just as an olive tree never sheds its leaves, neither in the winter nor in the summer. Just as the leaves and the olives are firmly attached to the tree, so too we will merit to see our own children firmly attached to their roots. They will be sitting firmly like olive trees around the table.

Furthermore, the husband will be blessed with blessings from above and from below, with wealth, with children and with grandchildren, as it is written "Behold, thus will be blessed the man who fears Hashem" (ibid.4) Zohar, Naso 125 Geder Olam, chapter 7.

I WILL ALWAYS PLACE HASHEM IN FRONT OF ME

The purpose of us being here on earth is to bring pleasure to HaShem. It manifests in the way we behave, in the way we dress, in the way we speak and in every aspect of our lives. We must always remember that we are doing it for HaShem, making sure that He is aware of it.

Whom did Avraham Avinu take with him during the sacrifice of Yitzchak? Avraham Avinu fulfills the most extreme devotion of self-sacrifice in Jewish History of Am Israel. During the sacrifice he was alone with HaKadosh Baruch Hu. He did not go and share the news with everyone.

It is told of Rabbi Shimshon Pincus זצק"ל who met in Switzerland a Jewish man who waited for a kidney transplant. The test revealed that Rabbi Pincus's kidney was a perfect match and the surgery was successfully performed.

Rabbi Pincus did not reveal to any of his friends, not even to his own family the loving kindness he performed with his body. He just notified them that he is being delayed for a few more weeks. He also asked the patient to keep it a secret.

Only when Rabbi Pincus passed away did this man who received the kidney come to comfort the family and revealed to them the great sacrifice the Rabbi made for him. This mitzvah was done between the Rabbi and HaShem with modesty.

THE DAUGHTER WHO HELPS HER MOTHER

The daughter who does kindnesses and does not share it with everyone is certainly befitting to be called "a modest daughter" who does her deeds in modesty.

It was told of a young boy, Baruch, whose parents had become observant. The parents sent Baruch to a Yeshiva, but as much as the father tried to find the time to help Baruch with his homework he was just too tired from working all day long. Baruch had a test and was not succeeding in learning for it himself and his father wasn't able to help.

They prayed to HaShem asking HaShem to help them to raise righteous children, telling the children tales about our sages. It was obvious they needed to do more.

The parents were trying to figure out how to help Baruch, they just didn't have the means to pay a teacher. Their 15 year old daughter would be married in a few years and if they had extra income they would certainly save it for her.

Miriam, Baruch's younger sister overheard the conversation and the next day she began to teach others. The parents were questioning whether they had failed in raising her, reminding their children that money is not everything and certainly it is possible to be content with little.

Here this is for you said Miriam, handing her recent salary to her mother. I know that Baruch needs a private teacher. Miriam took on additional jobs only to provide the extra assistance for her brother.

She organized a camp for children just before Passover, helping her mother until late hours of the night. Her mother promised Miriam that one day she would buy her a beautiful gift. Miriam's response was that she didn't need a gift, "it is a gift to see Baruch smile with contentment, it is a joy and such a pleasure to see him run to learn Torah, the teacher said he is doing much better. This is the most precious gift I can ever receive".

Once, while I was engrossed in my studies, my mother entered the study room. With tears in her eyes she revealed the sacrifice my sister had made for me, and about her personal money box which she used for my benefit.

This event was told by Baruch himself 15 years later. He grew up to be a scholar in Jewish studies, a Talmid Chacham. Often when I work on a difficult sugya (issue) and wrinkle my forehead while learning Gemara, in time, when I successfully managed to unravel a difficult question I remember my sister Miriam and know that all that I learn and become is hers. In her merit I am not a failure, I can unravel difficult questions from the Gemara.

What a loving kindness, with modesty, without telling any of her friends.

WHY DO WE NEED TO BE MODEST

Parashat Ki Teitzei -15, For HaShem, your God walks in the midst of your camp to rescue you and to deliver your enemies before you; so your camp shall be Holy, so that He will not see a shameful thing among you and turn away from behind you.

When our camp is holy, and we do not show immodesty as it is written in Parashat Ki Teitzei we merit Divine protection from HaShem Himself. HaShem will walk among us and protect us.

There are four places in the Torah which command us to be modest.

1. The Tabernacle was covered by three layers.

2. A Torah scholar must wear a long coat.

3. The Cohen Gadol must wear 8 articles of clothing.

4. The woman must dress modestly more than the man does.

WHY?

Rebbetzin Rivka Ketz explains brilliantly. Imagine that someone enters the Tabernacle and admires its beauty - the silver and gold vessels, amazing engraving, the enormous physical beauty which was invested in it; a person can be mistaken as to what his eye captures.

There is so much to see, we can easily forget the inner holiness of the Tabernacle. Here is the dwelling place of HaShem. The place where man can come very close to HaKadosh Baruch Hu.

The only reason we are so overwhelmed with its beauty comes from the deep inner holiness of the Tabernacle, the eye cannot possibly comprehend it fully, and therefore, fearing that man would miss the true point and the true purpose of our holy Tabernacle, we must cover it.

When someone is overwhelmed by the outer physical beauty of the Tabernacle - it can easily be mistaken as idol worshiping, because we often cannot differentiate between a holy place and any regular inanimate object. Therefore in order to emphasize its real and true beauty we must cover it. It will allow us to notice the inner holiness of the Tabernacle.

Our Mezuzah is always covered. The body is God's holy creation, the sacred house of the soul. The way we maintain our respect for the body is by keeping it covered. Not because it is shameful. But because it is so precious.

This is true for men's bodies too, and some laws of modest dress apply to them as well. However, the feminine body has a beauty and a power that far surpasses the masculine. The kabbalists teach that a woman's body has deeper beauty because her soul comes from a higher place. For this reason, her body must be kept discreetly covered.

In a world where the woman's body has been reduced to a cheap advertising gimmick, we need no proof for the truth of this wisdom. Where all is exposed, nothing is sacred. But that which is truly precious, we keep under wraps."

PARABLE BY THE BEN ISH CHAI

There was a king who had a rare tree, the king loved the tree very much and had enjoyed devoting his spare time nurturing, grooming, pampering and caring for the tree. He feared that one day someone would dig out the tree and take it away.

One day he called his most important minister and requested that the tree be covered, that way no one would be able to take the tree away. In addition the cover will protect the tree from the evil eye. The king had come to inspect the job that his minister had just finished. "The cover is too short" the king said. "The trunk is visible - although you did use a high quality cover".

The next day the minister proudly displayed the new cover - "The cover is transparent" exclaimed the king angrily. "The entire tree is visible! Why did you bother to cover it to start with"?

The following day when the king came to inspect the cover, the tree was covered in red. "The color is too noticeable!" said the king.

The moral of this story is that all the short, transparent and red coverings can't be called covers.

Everyone wondered what was going on under the red cover, so the minister covered it again with a tighter cover which revealed the shape of the leaf.

Then what is the purpose of covering it? Asked the king. The minister then painted a picture of the tree on the cover so everyone can clearly see the tree is hidden under the cover.

The angry minister snapped, why do you need to cover the tree to start with? The tree is so beautiful why not impress everyone with its beauty?

Because I commanded you to cover the tree, replied the king.

The moral of the story is that everyone chooses to cover their hair the way they feel like. The question is what do they really cover? HaShem asked women to cover their hair and their bodies. They cover their hair in red, tight, transparent, short covers, even with someone else's hair.

At the end of the day the women realize that they really don't need to cover their hair. The women of our current generation saying, we are beautiful women we would like to be noticed, why do we have to cover our beauty? Why should we cover ourselves? The answer to this question is that it is what HaShem asked us to do.

If you wore a see through jacket, even if it covered up to your neckline and to your wrist, it would have defeated the purpose because it reveals that which is uncovered and exposed.

A MODEST WOMAN

Her inner beauty shines through, King David said in Tehillim chapter 45:14, the entire honor and glory which is due to a daughter of the King comes from within.

It doesn't matter whether she wears a beautiful crown or expensive clothing, her true essence is being the daughter of a King. There is no greater honor than to be a daughter of a King.

MODESTY IN SPEECH

HaShem created the world with speech, He spoke and it came into being. That means that our words are very important and they can build our homes, our lives and our world or God forbid destroy everything we built and created.

MODESTY IN DRESS

Clothing has a tremendous impact on a person. Our sages say that the Kohanim (high priests) were infused with holiness during their priesthood duties only when they wear their special garments.

Without them they couldn't perform their duties. The Kohen had special garments to fulfill his duties at the Temple. He possessed a special holiness while wearing those special clothes. The holiness of the high priest stayed with him as long as he was wearing those special clothes.

A daughter of Israel receives holiness as she fulfills her own duties as HaShem's daughter; our sages compare the importance and modesty of her clothing to those of the Kohen Gadol the high priest.

Sefer HaChinuch speaks about how our actions follow our heart, and naturally we behave differently when we are modest, our speech and our manners are more refined. We act, speak and behave as HaShem's daughters.

Our friend once invited a young woman and her girlfriend for Shabbat. He was trying to introduce one of the girls to his friend. After dinner the young man told his friend that he liked the more modest girl and not the one who was very pretty and came with noticeable makeup and tight clothing.

RABBI NEUGROSCHEL

It is told of a woman who came to shake Rabbi Neugroschel's hand. She and her husband were deeply hurt by his lack of respect by not extending his hand. The Rabbi explained that a Jewish woman is a daughter of a King. My wife he continued is just like your wife, they are both daughters of HaKadosh Baruch Hu. Not everyone can come to a Queen and touch her; not everyone can even come close to her, and that shows respect to the Queen. It shows that she belongs to someone else and not everyone can just touch her whenever he feels like. A woman can bring holiness to every day and every minute by being modest and turn her home into a small sanctuary.

THE STORY OF THE SHORT CHILD

There was a couple who had a short son. They were debating whether to administer the growth hormones to help him grow taller. There are many side effects in the growth hormone and so they asked the Dr. whether she would have given those pills to her own son? She said that in her world the physical appearance is very important so she probably would have, however in your world she said the physical appearance has a lesser significance. Your son will be judged on other qualities, so in this case, if I were in your place I would have not taken the risk.

The truth of the matter is that it is the inner self which shines through and not the splendor of the physical appearance which captures the eye. We should also remember that our physical appearance is temporary; the inner beauty is a lasting beauty.

LEZCHUT ALL KLAL ISRAEL
#1-REWARD FOR MODESTY

I heard a beautiful story in a shiur given by Rabbi Avrohom M. Alter שליט"א. He told the story in the name of Rebbetzin Kanievsky.

In March, someone packed a car with 100 kilos of explosives and parked it at the Cinemall in Haifa. It was parked near a supporting pillar. Had it exploded, not only would it have destroyed that pillar, but other cars in the lot would have caught fire causing the gas tanks to explode. In that very popular mall, the consequences would have been too horrendously tragic to contemplate.

The explosion did not happen. A passerby spotted some smoke coming from the car and alerted the police who sent specialists and they were able to come and defuse the explosives.

Even Ehud Olmert (Former Prime Minister of Israel) recognized this was a miracle, although he attributed it to the alertness of civilians.

Here's what really happened:

Several weeks before this event, a girl in Haifa went for tests at the hospital and her parents were told she had stomach cancer. The tumor was very large, it had metastasized and there was nothing the doctors could do. They told her to go home to die.

This non-religious girl and her non-religious parents pleaded with the doctors to try. They begged them at least to make an effort. The doctors finally agreed and told her to come back the next day for surgery.

She was assigned a young, inexperienced surgeon. They felt it would be good practice for him, and since there was nothing that could help her, it didn't really matter.

The night before the surgery, this non-religious girl pleaded with HaShem. She said to Him, "HaKadosh Baruch Hu, when we had the Beit HaMikdash (our Holy Temple) people could bring you sacrifices to plead their case. Now we have no priests, we have no Beit HaMikdash.

"But I still want to bring you a sacrifice" she said to HaShem. She went to her closet and took out all her immodest clothing and took it out to the yard and burned them. As her clothes went up in flames, she cried out, "This is my korban."

The next day this girl went to the hospital in her nightgown, she had burned her entire wardrobe and this was all she had left. She had the surgery. The tumor had not metastasized, as was previously believed. It was totally contained. It was easily removed. And it was benign.

She told all her non-religious friends about the miracle. When the girl had recovered enough to get out of bed, her friends brought over all their immodest clothing and made another fire.

Left with nothing to wear, the girls needed new clothes. When that bomb was supposed to explode at the Cinemall, these girls were inside buying themselves new, modest clothing.

Depending on what eyes we are looking through…

Is it a coincidence that a civilian saw some smoke?

Or a miracle reward for Tzniut (modesty)?

"After I read this, HaShem gave me a great thought. Let's all get together and make a bonfire, and pray to HaShem to accept our wigs as korban for us personally and all of Klal Yisrael for Refuah (full recovery), Yesha (rescue), Bracha (blessing), Hatzlacha (good luck), Parnassa (livelihood), Shidduchim (marriage match), Shalom Bayit (peace in the home), and for the Geula (redemption)".

WE MUST NOT DEVIATE FROM THE VERDICT OUR SAGES ANNOUNCED EITHER FROM THE RIGHT OR FROM THE LEFT

HaShem commanded us to do the right thing and we must obey His command. HaShem had commanded us to listen to our sages. In Deuteronomy 17:11 "You shall act in accordance with instructions given to you and the ruling that was handed down to you, you must not deviate from the verdict that they announced to you either to the right or to the left."

"The Gedolei Hador (our sages) had stated that today's wigs are not a suitable head covering, creating confusion whether the woman is married or not. This very action creates an obstacle.

Rabbi Ovadia Yosef זצ"ל said we were asked by HaShem to listen to our sages, and they forbid wearing wigs. People often ask why davka modesty is so important, every mitzvah is as important.

We must keep in mind that when HaShem created the woman He said twice that with every limb and organ of her body she must be modest. How can a woman stand in HaShem's presence and fulfill the mitzvah of lighting the Shabbat candles dressed immodestly with the most impure wig on top of her head. How can a husband say Kiddush in front of this woman? This is why the other good deeds follow the mitzvah of modesty.

Similar to a person who does mitzvot and eats unkosher food, how can he fulfill the mitzvot with a confused mind and a impure body? The Torah clearly states that a non kosher food confuses the mind and defiles the body? A woman's creation and her essence, substance and true nature are the most important...

STORY OF RABBI'S SON

There is a story about a Rabbi who came to observe his son and his classmates climbing a tree. Each child had to reach the top of the tree and each child fell down before reaching the top of the tree. The only one who made it to the top was the Rabbi's son. "How did you succeed? Asked the Rabbi, and your classmates did not?" The son pointed out that the entire time he was climbing the tree he only looked up; his friends on the other hand looked down. When we focus on our destination, our aim and purpose, we prevail, and then it is much easier to reach our goal.

A STORY ABOUT A KING'S SON

The Midrash on Song of Songs (5:2) says "open up for me an opening the size of an eye of the needle and in turn I will enlarge it to be an opening through which a wagon can enter." God just needs an opening as big as an eye of the needle. If you take the initiative and allow God to enter into your life through a tiny hole, you'll see exponentially greater outcome in all you do.

There is a story about a king's son who left his home, he wandered for years until he came to a faraway land. His father the king, longing for his only son sent his royal staff to find him.

The son did not wish to make the long and grueling trip back home. The king's advisers were told by the king to let the son know that if he comes towards him 80 percent, his father the king will come the remaining 20 percent. If the son comes toward his father 50 percent the father will come toward his son the remaining 50 percent.

The king's only request was that the son would make a small effort and he the king will come the rest of the way for his son. The King of the Universe said to us, you come toward Me a small distance and I will assist you with the rest. It doesn't matter what we cover our heads with, we can place a silly hat on our head or a clown's hat or a strange hat or a wig and we will fulfill the mitzvah of covering our heads but NOT the mitzvah of modesty.

THE STORY OF A FIRE WITH A MORAL LESSON

A story is told about a Rabbi who informed his students of a fire outside the classroom. He warned his students to remain inside. "My dear students he addressed his class: no one can cross the marked line and open the door to see me." One of his students however came running outside, did I not warn you not to open the door asked the Rabbi? I didn't come out from the door replied the student, I jumped from the window.

The Rabbi said not to open the door and the student said he exited through the window.

Similar to a woman who covers her head with all kinds of inappropriate head coverings.

Similar to a child's play, I did not come out from the door I came out from the window. It is important to understand that when a woman insists on covering her head with a wig, it totally and completely defeats the purpose of head covering. Do you really think that HaKadosh Baruch Hu asked us women to cover our hair with hair? Does it make any sense?

The hair is Erva, the same as pubic hair. In this case how can a wig with other women's hair be an option to hair cover?

It is similar to the kid who came out of the window. You are missing the point. You are missing the bottom line. We are not permitted to reveal any hair.

Because the hair makes the woman more beautiful, men can think that the woman is not married, the point is that the woman should not look like she is single. A man can only look at a woman when he is looking for a Shidduch.

By wearing a wig a man can think she is not married and he can then easily stumble, by her causing him to think she is not married.

Today when a woman buys a wig it has to look like her own hair. It is a transgression because the mitzvah of head covering is for the woman not to look single. She must look married. The woman is missing the point, she is saying to HaShem: look at me, I cover my hair. When in reality you are not, you have someone else's hair on your head, obviously it isn't a head cover, completely ignoring the Divine purpose and request.

When a woman covers her hair with a scarf then she will actually look like a married woman and not like the kid who came out of the window and missed the point.

Did you ever see one Arab woman with a wig? They look more modest than our daughters.

Did our foremothers wear a wig?

Obviously it is a way of life in which the nations of the world adapted and not what HaShem intended of His Chosen daughters.

Did Rivka our foremother cover her hair with a wig when she saw Yitzchak or did she cover her head and face with a scarf in order that Yitzchak would not look at her physical beauty and will be able to see her inner beauty?

Yehuda never saw the face of his daughter in law, her hair and face were always covered with a scarf so when he saw her on the road totally uncovered he did not recognize her.

The Rabbis in Europe had no choice but to allow Jewish women to wear a wig during the pogroms and times of great danger. It was important for the Jewish women to look like the non-Jewish women to avoid being killed. It was supposed to last only until the danger passed.

There was no logical reason to continue the practice when there was no more danger.

We must differentiate between a custom and a law. A custom is a ritual we adopted from our family, such as eating rice on Passover, or men from different Chasidut groups who dress differently. That doesn't mean that they have a different Torah or different prayers or that they keep Shabbat differently. It only means that they adopted customs from their family which they use today.

On the other hand a Divine Law cannot be changed.

Therefore, the law of covering one's head with a scarf is eternal and cannot be changed. The Shulchan Aruch the Code of Jewish Law clearly states that we are not to follow in the way of the nations.

RABBANIT RUTH MENASHE Z"L WROTE

Chacham Yosef Chaim a"h, writes in his book Keter Malchut that Hanukkah is one very special day where women are endowed with a higher level of Kedusha (sanctity), in the same way as they are on Rosh Chodesh the new month.

Rashi explains in the Gemara of Shabbat (23a), that women were the ones who brought about the miracle of Hanukkah and therefore, are obligated to hear the blessings on Hanukkah candles. The Ben Ish Chai adds that women should not wear their everyday clothing, but rather, should change into festive attire and if they own gold jewelry, they should wear it.

I would like to tell you about one courageous lady - Hannah, the daughter of Mattityahu, the High Priest. The Midrash relates that Hannah got married at a time when every single bride was forced to go to the Greek official before being allowed back to her husband.

Many Jewish women did not get married in order to avoid this devastating decree. This lasted three years and eight months. Hannah, in the midst of her wedding celebration, and in the presence of honored quests exposed herself. Imagine the embarrassment of her groom, her family and her father-in-law! Her brothers wanted to kill her. At that moment she spoke up and claimed: "You are enraged that I am standing naked here in your presence, but you have kept quiet all this time while Jewish brides are being defiled by the Greeks? This resulted in the rebellion of the Maccabim (her brothers) against the Greeks.

There are times when we have to "go with the flow". However, there are times when we have to go against the tide. It may be ironic, that Hannah had to remove her clothes in order to make a change or bring about the onset of the rebellion.

I wonder whether in our days, going against the tide requires us to do the exact opposite: cover ourselves more. This is perhaps a message for the righteous women of our generation.

The more the people around us expose their bodies and infuse impurity into the world, the more we need to infuse holiness into the world by raising the bar of our modesty through the way we are dressed and how we cover ourselves.

The Jewish nation has always been the victim of foreign influences.

The Babylonians, the Greeks, the Romans, they all wanted to confuse us and to make us assimilate among the nations.

Many Jews fell, but those who were God fearing stood strong and remained Jews. They kept all the mitzvot exactly as they kept them for thousands of years.

MAKING A DECISION

When the New Year approaches we make resolutions to cover our heads. Why do so many women have good intentions but don't follow through? Why are we inspired to change but can lose the excitement so quickly?

There are many explanations, one of them is taken from the Ethics of Our Fathers – that of pretending to study the Torah which we can apply to head covering. Do not say that in the future I will make the decision to cover my head, for perhaps you will miss the opportunity. Good decisions need to be acted upon immediately.

It has been shown that intellectual theories or emotional feelings that do not have an immediate action dissipate quickly. The next time you are inspired to cover your hair don't put it off any longer, do it now!

As we all know there are sparks of Kedusha (holiness) in clothing which are worn by their owners. Just as food can affect the soul, the clothing we wear can affect our soul just the same.

There is a story in the book Shomer Emunim about a Rabbi who visited the Baal Shem Tov during Yom Kippur. He used the Baal Shem Tov's kittel (robe). As soon as he put on the clothing of the Holy Baal Shem Tov he was covered by such a great and enormous reverence that he had to be put to bed. It seemed the Rabbi had lost consciousness but with great effort his life was saved.

How much so hair which grew on a gentile woman with her genetic code which includes her spiritual traits? The same hair which accompanied her during her immodest and defiled actions and more so in the event that the same hair was used for idol worshiping.

Think about all the impurity and abomination the wearer of this wig creates on herself and on her head. This impurity attaches itself to the woman who wears this wig. Through wearing this wig an impurity of spirit attaches itself to the woman.

What about an immodest woman who gave her hair to be used for a wig and she has had illnesses or mental problems? Is this something HaShem's daughter would want to place on her head? What about a dead woman's hair?

It is similar to a woman who says, why do I have to go to the mikvah (the ritual bath). I can use my bath tub. No! You can't! You can put bleach in the bathtub and all the cleaning soaps you can think of, you will never be spiritually clean.

The same with a wig. You can clean the hair. Sterilize the hair. Put bleach on the hair - it doesn't matter! All the problems, the health issues, the immodest actions, her bad energy, her speech, are attached to this wig whether we like it or not!

Whether we choose to acknowledge it or not, this is something we need to think about before covering our heads with someone else's impurities and problems.

SOMETHING TO HIDE

Arron Moss answered a question about why does Judaism tell women to keep their bodies covered? Is there something shameful about a woman's body? Why should a woman have to hide herself just so others shouldn't be tempted? Here is his answer in the weekly reader Scroll Chabad.org February 1, 2013.

You are assuming that the reason for modest dress is to avoid men's temptation. However, the Jewish value of modest dress is not merely about how women are viewed by others.

Covering something doesn't always mean being ashamed of it. Have you ever noticed how we treat a Torah scroll?

We never leave it lying around. It is kept inside a synagogue, in the ark, behind a curtain, wrapped in a mantle, held tightly closed with a belt.
It is taken out only when it is to be used for a holy purpose, to be read during the prayer service. As soon as we have finished reading from it, we immediately wrap it up again and put it away.
Why do we go to such trouble to conceal the Torah? Are we ashamed of it? Is there something to hide?

Of course not. Because the Torah is our holiest object, because it is so sacred and special and precious, we never leave it exposed unnecessarily. We keep it under wraps because we don't want to treat it lightly; we don't want to become too casual with it. Were the Torah to be always open and visible, it might become too familiar and its sanctity minimized. By bringing it out only when needed, we maintain our reverence and respect for the Torah.

The body is God's Holy creation, the sacred house of the soul. The way we maintain our respect for the body is by keeping it covered.

Not because it is shameful. But because it is so precious.

This is true for men's bodies too, and laws of modest dress apply to them as well.

However, the feminine body has a beauty and a power that far surpasses the masculine. The Kabbalists teach that a woman's body has a deeper beauty because her soul comes from a higher place. For this reason, her body must be kept discreetly covered.

In a world where the woman's body has been reduced to a cheap advertising gimmick; we need no proof for the truth of this wisdom.

Where all is exposed, nothing is sacred. But that which is truly precious, we keep under wraps.

Areyala Savir, a young blind Israeli singer from Tzfat, had a four month old son, comprehensive testing revealed an awful scenario - a tumor was in her son's liver.

Concerned, Areyala's husband sought the advice of a Rabbi.

The Rabbi's advice was that he put on Tefillin and keep Shabbat and that Areyala his wife would take on the mitzvah of lighting Shabbat candles, keep family purity and cover her hair.

The husband took upon himself to keep Shabbat and put on the Tefillin, his wife accepted the mitzvah of lighting the candles and keeping family purity, however, head covering was just too demanding for her.

Standing by her son's bedside and thinking about the Rabbis request a thought came to her mind.

Being a poet and a songwriter she re-positioned the letters on the words כיסוי לראש (head covering) and a new word emerged, סיכוי לאושר (a chance towards happiness). She decided to cover her hair and Baruch HaShem her son merited to make a complete recovery.

The Torah and Mitzvot we do are our badge of conquest, our symbol of triumph. It is well known that our generation's modesty ethics are in an all-time low. The nations of the world are dictating how we must look and dress. We are just like the sheep following the shepherd, following in their footsteps.

The Chafetz Chaim emphasizes the importance of keeping the law of modesty. There is a reward that awaits a woman who keeps the law of modesty. When a woman is modest in her behavior she will merit that her children will grow up to become Torah scholars.

I would like to share with you the hidden secret that lies beneath this most mighty mitzvah. It is the issue of submission.

On a personal level, when a woman subdues or restricts her will and desires; being disciplined is the direction of self-power moving her closer towards more refined character!

We are thus able to elevate ourselves and become the true Jewish mate to our spouses. As it states in Mishlei (Proverbs) 12:4 - The powerful woman is the crown of her husband.

Covering our head is one way that shows our creator that we are willing to thank Him for all He does for us and will do for us in the future. How are we going to be rewarded? Hashem rewards us by protecting us and placing the Shechinah the presence of Hashem above us. We do something little for Hashem and we are rewarded with something big from Hashem himself.

Regretfully, women take pride in showing off their hair to look beautiful, not realizing that as long as they look beautiful for HaShem it is all that matters. After all, all the blessings come from HaShem.

The inclination is very persistent in this matter. A woman is willing to do all the other Mitzvot except this one. However, it shows submission to the Creator.

The one who lowers himself before our Maker is lifted up by HaKadosh Baruch Hu Himself. We have sacred secrets in our possession: subdue yourself for HaShem and watch in wonder the many gates of heaven that will open up before you.

A woman who covers her hair does a mitzvah every second, why lose such an opportunity? A head covering for a woman is a mitzvah from the Torah so when she doesn't cover her hair she desecrates the commandment every minute.

What is the definition of the word "modest"? It is covered, not revealed, hidden, and concealed. The opposite of modesty is exposed, revealed, and open. We fail to do the easy mitzvot. However, Hashem desires those more than the more difficult ones.

There is nothing in the world that can protect you like a mitzvah. In the merit of this mighty mitzvah of head covering, as long as we have our head covering on, we create an angel to protect us.

Where else can we do something so little and be rewarded with seeing and being with the Shechinah, the presence of Hashem?

Our sages gave a parable in the Gemara of the king asking his servants to bring him a handful of sand and a handful of gold.

When they fail to bring him either one, whom do you think will incur the king's anger? The one who failed to bring the sand or the one who failed to bring the gold? Of course, the one who failed to bring the sand since it is readily available. Gold, on the other hand, is harder to obtain.

It is written in the book of Numbers chapter 5:18 and Devarim 23:15 (Isha Sota). This passage deals with a woman who behaved in an unseemly manner, giving her husband good reason to suspect her of adultery, but there is no proof of either guilt or innocence.

The Kohen uncovers her hair, while making her move from place to place in the doorway of the Courtyard of the Mikdash, then he places the offering on her outstretched palms to humiliate and tire her - all in the hope that if she is guilty she will confess.

Since the verse takes it for granted that her head was covered until the Kohen uncovered the woman's head, the Sages derive that it is disgraceful for a married woman to be seen bareheaded (Rashi).

A woman's concern is for her physical beauty. However, King Solomon said (Proverbs 31:30) falsehood is grace and vanity is beauty and that only God fearing woman will be praised. HaGaon MeVelna explained that it means that beauty alone without fear of Heaven is vain.

I once asked my friend from Five Towns in New York to introduce a young woman to a young man I knew who was looking for a Shidduch. She told me that in her Synagogue she cannot tell who is married and who isn't because the women wear wigs, those wigs look so real she cannot tell whether its a wig or their own hair.

The women who are married must look differently; a man should be able to tell immediately if this woman is married or not...

Being observant women is understanding that the most important relationship you have is your personal relationship with HaShem - nothing else matters. However, we must keep in mind that the mitzvot we do are the ones that bring us closer to HaShem. The head covering mitzvah especially, because by covering your hair you are saying to HaShem that you want a relationship with Him.

That the crown on your head is a symbol of your being a Bat Melech, a daughter of HaShem. A daughter who proudly wears His crown to place HaShem on top of your head and on top of your priorities at all times.

OPEN UP FOR ME AN OPENING THE SIZE OF A NEEDLE

The Gemara says that if we try to come closer to HaShem, even if we begin with a small step towards teshuva, HaShem will help us the rest of the way. We even need HaShem to help us build a closer relationship with Him.

MODESTY, THE HONOR AND BEAUTY OF A KING'S DAUGHTER

Each one of you is a unique daughter to HaShem.

Did you know that the Jewish people had prophetesses? We have heard of Elijah, Shmuel and Yechezkel the prophets, however Sarah, Miriam, Deborah and Esther were our prophetesses too.

Looking into our History we can clearly see that the salvation came to the Jewish people from women. We came out of Egypt in the merit of righteous women, and in the future we will be redeemed by righteous women.

The miracle of Hanukkah occurred by Yehudit, the daughter of Yochanan the high priest. She cut off the head of the top Greek general winning the battle. It was all in her merit.

Queen Esther was the main player in the miracle of Purim.

The women do have an honorable position in Judaism; if we take advantage of our strength we can reach the top of the mountain.

The question is asked how is it possible? A woman doesn't go to Beit Midrash to learn Torah, she doesn't put on Tefillin, nor Tzizit, she is not required to go to Shul, so what makes her such an important and influential person? How can a woman reach the level of a prophetess?

HaShem had given the woman a good gift; modesty He called it. All her strength and power stand upon the pillar of modesty. The more she invests in her modesty the more she elevates and sanctifies her soul, until she reaches the level of prophecy.

WHAT IS HIDDEN BEHIND THE MITZVAH OF TZNIUT

To our dear daughters of Israel, HaShem chose you to be the precious jewel and diamond of the Jewish nation. And just as a precious Jewel is not displayed and left alone for every seeker and inspector to observe, so is our precious and holy body which must be covered and modest from any foreign lookers and strangers. It should be kept for the one who is the most precious to you - your husband.

WHAT IS OUR HOLIEST OBJECT

Remember that the holiest object which we possess is our Torah Scroll. Where do we keep the Torah Scroll? We keep it in a special ark. HaShem considers our body as holy as the " Torah Scroll" and our clothing as the "Ark". He asks us to be a modest woman wearing modest clothing.

WHAT IS THE ESSENCE OF A WOMAN?

Modesty is the essence of a woman; it is her honor, her dignity, and her true beauty.

A Jewish child is like a "Torah Scroll", he is placed in the "Ark" which is our womb - our holy body. We as women are chosen to do this exalted and awesome job... The woman is the only one who navigates the purity in the home.

Only because a woman is on such a high and exalted level HaShem commanded her to keep the mitzvah of modesty which is the tool from which the woman is sanctified and earns her high spiritual position. Is there anything more exalted than that?

WHY DO OUR SAGES CALL THE MODEST WOMAN A HOME AND A WALL

Just as if there is a breach, an opening, a loophole in the wall and through them danger can enter into the home, the same is when there is a breach, an opening and a loophole in modesty. A modest woman protects her entire home. The more the woman is punctilious in her modesty the more efficient is her home.

Eshet Chayil (Proverbs 31:10-31)

Strength and majesty are her garments, she joyfully awaits the last day. What does it mean?

The woman who dresses modestly, a woman who does it with strength and majesty without being embarrassed in the presence of family and friends, a woman who does it only for the sole purpose of bringing honor to HaShem in spite of it being difficult, will joyfully receive her reward with nachat, simcha and laughter.

The same grace she acquired by not being modest will now be rewarded with abundance of blessings from above and below.

Remember, when a husband sees immodestly dressed women, it does affect his thoughts; it isn't a secret that it affects his love toward his wife.

It is identical to the destruction of the Temple, just like the destruction of our homes can cause separation of the family unit, so can a modest women prevent this kind of destruction and separation. In my lifetime I met many such couples. Who caused this situation to occur? An immodestly dressed woman.

Elana Roth, a Rabbanit who lived in America and moved to Israel wrote about the Kaballistic outlook on head covering in Tevet 5765 (2005). On a simple level of understanding one will hear that a married woman needs to cover her hair because hair is one of the most appealing aspects of a woman. Hair is her beauty and her distinctly feminine look compared to a man.

The explanation goes on to say that, therefore, one must cover her hair in order to not entice the lust of men! But do men have no control over their desires?

If one has ever been in an observant community, one knows the level Torah observant men will take to ensure there are absolutely no inappropriate exchanges in speech or action with a woman.

So if married women are covering their hair so as to be less appealing to men, why then are wigs accepted as a head covering in observant circles? Why aren't women just required to wear head scarves?

Sephardi women are not promoted to cover their heads with a wig. A wig can be extremely beautiful and appealing on women.

For this reason a woman who dresses immodestly loses the peace at home, measure for measure. Don't contribute to the destruction of the Jewish homes in Israel. Be modest!

Just as you take upon yourself to dress modestly and sacrifice for others, so will HaShem make sure that you will merit a true peaceful home of high standards, and pleasure from your husband and children. Is there a more enormous blessing then this?

GEMARA SUKKAH 53

A personal Divine protection on Klal Israel is the reward of modesty in clothing. We are protected from problems and illnesses.

THE LOOK ALIKE SHEITEL

Some wigs are impossible to discern.

It's hard to tell whether it's your own hair or a wig.

Many times, I cannot tell the difference.

I remember when wigs were suspected to have idol worshiping rituals.

We believe that nothing happens by chance.

Everything has been predestined above.

So the question is asked - why did HaShem do this?

What is HaShem trying to say?

Why did He bring this phenomenon upon us?

Why did He cause these events to happen?

What does he want to teach us?

We are a holy nation, bearing the single truth in the entire world—(there is only one truth).

Our mission is to be a light to the nations.

Hide your hair. Hide your physical beauty to reveal your inner beauty, so that you are more treasured, so that you are more modest, hidden and respected...

Our physical beauty is temporary – the inner beauty is everlasting.

Our Torah is eternal.

The same rules of modesty that existed thousands of years ago still exist today.

Fashion is a gentile concept and we were specifically commanded not to follow in the ways of other Nations, not in dress and not in behavior.

Today even if Elijah the prophet appears and tries to convince me that a wig is modest I will not believe him.

GO LEARN THE SUBJECT OF HEAD COVERING

I believe wholeheartedly that everyone who questions the modesty of a wig should check thoroughly on the subject. Why must we rely on opinions and rumor? It is very important to check the subject matter and not jump to conclusions based on what others are doing.

ALL OF OUR SAGES WARNED NOT TO WEAR A WIG

They are saying if the head cover looks like hair then it is hair. It is the same as if a woman has no hair covering on. HaGaon Rabbi Tzvi Ordentlech added that it is forbidden to sell wigs. He was very strict about it.

He said that Rabbis who allow their wives to wear wigs are not great Rabbis. He said that everyone who wears a wig sins, and that it is preferable to go without a wig then with it.

PEAH NOCHRIT - A FOREIGN GENTILE WIG

Our sages are saying that just by the name itself one can learn that wigs are not for our Jewish daughters. They are meant to be used by gentiles. I have yet to see an Arab woman with a wig, interesting, their head covering is according to our Halacha Code of Law.

Hagaon Rabbi Shalom Shevdron makes a point that there is no Posek Halacha Adjudicators or a great Rabbi that will give permission for a daughter of Israel to look like a single woman.

Hagaon Rabbi Ben Tzion Mutzafi said that the wigs of today are extremely immodest. For those who say that they are preferable, they are confused and confusing others, our foremothers covered their hair only with a scarf.

It is repulsive to place on our head and brain the hair of a non jewish woman. To place on the head of HaShem's daughter the gentile woman's illnesses, all her troubles, her idol worshiping, her pritzut (immodesty), her licentiousness and who knows what else, and light the Shabbat candles in honor of our Holy Shabbat with this abomination on her head. How shameful it is to stand before HaShem and ask for mercy.

HaShem our Father in heaven who clearly disapproves and does not like His holy daughters to wear this impurity on their heads.

Hagaon our sage Rabbi Yehuda Tzadka said that it is preferable that the women who wear a wig remove the wig. Her own hair would be preferable... This makes sense since a wig is not considered to be a head covering for our precious and holy daughters of Israel.

Haadmor Milaluv said that it is much preferable that the men will cut their beards and peyot then that their wives wear wigs.

When parents approached Hagaon Rabbi Shimon Cherari for a shidduch match blessing, he wanted to know first what the young woman would wear after her marriage. If they said a scarf he would give them a blessing and if they said a wig he would stop the conversation immediately. There is only one way to cover our heads and it is only by a scarf, a wig is not negotiable.

We must keep in mind that the Rabbis who permitted women to wear wigs, were not given the liberty to change Halacha, the Jewish Code of Law, they only did so to save lives during the persecutions and danger, and it was not supposed to last forever.

How do we know? We know because the European Jews were the only ones who were given temporary approval until the danger passed. All the other women from all the Arab countries are and were forbidden to wear wigs, they covered their head and looked just like the Arab women did and did not need the temporary verdict to change to a wig.

Hagaon Rabbi Ben Tzion Abba Shaul said during a Shabbat lecture, that it is forbidden to wear a wig in public.

Hagaon Rabbi Avraham Yeshaya Karelitz (Hachazon Ish) said that the issue of a wig is very disturbing to him, it is certainly not modest and it is something that our daughters learned from our non-Jewish neighbors and then the illness spread to our orthodox homes.

When seeing a woman wearing the old fashioned wig Hagaon Rabbi Yosef Chaym Zonnenfeld said to the woman, it is difficult to say that you look completely immodest, you just look similar to the non-Jewish women.

What does it mean? It means that our daughters are not supposed to wear wigs. Period! Not even the old fashioned ones.

Hagaon HaRav Elazer Man Shach said in a speech to the Yeshiva students: it is urgent for me to say to you that the existence of the Kolelim (Torah study place) depends on your wives head covering. If your wives wear wigs we must close the Kolelim.

Hagaon Rabbi Yitzchak Ratzabi said in a lecture it is forbidden to allow our Jewish daughters to wear wigs. Look closely and see all the obstacles which such a family endures. The dissolution of families and homes. I am against all wigs, it is a severe disregard of modesty.

Rabbi Ben Tzion Shafier (The Shmuz) The Jewish Press June 2018 Parashat Korach.

"And Korach, son of Yizhar, son of Kehat, son of Levi, and Datan and Aviram, sons of Eliav, together with Ohn, son of Pelet, sons of Reuvain." – Bamidbar 16:1

Korach was not chosen for a position as head of his shevet (tribe). He felt entitled to it, and his jealousy drove him to rebel against Moshe and HaShem.

Recognizing that he couldn't stand alone, he gathered two hundred and fifty leaders of the nation, and they swore their allegiance to Korach and his cause.

The plan was to depose Moshe as leader of the Jewish people, and instead appoint Korach. In the end, their rebellion failed, and every man, woman, and child was swallowed by the ground.

Of this group, only one man survived: Ohn, son of Pelet. The Midrash explains that it was his wife who saved him. She said to him, "What do you gain from all of this? If Moshe wins, you are but a lackey. And if Korach wins you are still but a lackey."

Her logic penetrated his heart. "You are right," he said, "but what can I do? I took an oath to remain loyal to the group. They will come tomorrow to get me, and I will be forced to join them."

His wife said, "Listen to my advice. I will stand outside our tent and uncover my hair. These are all holy men. When they see a woman not properly attired, they will run away."

She then gave him enough wine to drink until he fell asleep drunk, and she tied him to the bed. Early the next morning, she went outside, uncovered her hair, and waited. When the first members of Korach's party came to bring Ohn to the demonstration, they saw a woman with her hair uncovered outside his tent. They immediately walked away. She remained there throughout the day. No man dared come to the tent. Then the time came for the standoff. When Korach's men were standing together, they were swallowed up alive, but Ohn was not amongst them. This is a fulfillment of the verse, "A wise woman builds her house…" (Daat Zakainim)

HOW COULD THEY HAVE BEEN SO FOOLISH?

This Daat Zakainim is very difficult to understand. Korach's group were men of great piety. The Torah calls them "leaders of the nation, men of reputation." And here we see an example of how careful they were in regards to mitzvah observance. Even though Ohn played a pivotal role in their cause, the mere sight of a woman with her hair uncovered made them run away. So how could these great people do something so egregious as to rebel against HaShem and His chosen representative?

The answer to this question can best be understood when we focus on the impossibility of free will.

When HASHEM took the neshama and put it into this world, it was to give man the opportunity to make himself into what he will be for eternity. The essence of our purpose here is to choose what is right and proper and to turn away from what is wrong and evil.

The problem, however, is that those options are set far apart and leave little choice. No thinking person would deliberately choose for himself a path of destruction. Every mitzvah helps us grow. Every sin damages us. HASHEM warned us to do this and not to do that because it is good for us and will benefit us for eternity. So how does man have free will? He will choose good and only good — because it's so clearly in his best interest.

To allow for free will, HaShem put the brilliant neshama into a body that clouds its vision and darkens its sight. The desires and inclinations of the body don't remain separate from me. They are mixed into my very essence and play out in my conscious mind. When I open my eyes in the morning, it isn't my body that wants to just lie there unmoving – I am lazy. At lunch, it isn't my stomach that cries out for food – I am hungry.

I am both the brilliant neshama and the base animal instinct. And so, I want to live a life of meaning, and I want to live completely for the moment. I want to be good, proper and noble, and I just don't care. I want this and I want that. Which one is the real me? The answer is both. And I am constantly changing, constantly in flux. Because these desires come from within me, they also distort my vision. When I desire something, my vision can become so blinded that I can hotly pursue something damaging to me, and not only fail to see the danger involved, but even begin to see it as an ultimate good.

THE DARKNESS OF PHYSICALITY
THE MESILLAT YESHARIM (PEREK 4)
EXPLAINS THIS WITH A PARABLE

Imagine a man walking at night on an unlit country road. Because of the darkness, he is in danger of tripping. There are, however, two types of hazards he faces. The first is that he won't see the pit in front of him, and he will fall in without even realizing the peril. The second danger, however, is more severe. The darkness can fool him so that he sees an object, but mistakes it for something else. He may look at a pillar in the distance and see it as a man. Or he might see a man and mistake him for a pillar. This menace is more severe because even if he were to be alert to the risk, he would ignore the warning signs because he sees with his own eyes that there is no danger.

Physicality is like the darkness of night. It blinds a person and doesn't allow him to see the danger in front of him. There are two types of mistakes that it causes. The first is that it doesn't allow him to see the hazard. He will continue on a path of life that is self-destructive, and he won't even recognize where he is headed until he is too far down the road to change course.

The second mistake, however, is far more dangerous. It is when man is so fooled by the darkness of physicality that he sees the good as if it were bad and the bad as if it were good. At this point, warning a man about the danger is useless. He sees it, but views it as something virtuous. And so, he will clutch to evil against all warnings and against all wisdom because in his blindness, it appears as good.

KORACH AND HIS CONGREGATION

This seems to be the answer to Korach and his people. They were Torah scholars, and they were holy Jews. And yet, they were blind. Korach was blinded by jealousy. He then presented arguments and proofs to the two hundred and fifty men that Moshe was making up his own set of rules. He was dynamic and convincing. Once the group accepted Korach's version of reality, they held fast to it. And then even the threat of a gruesome death didn't faze them.

It wasn't that they didn't see the danger. They did. But they saw it as scare tactic, a way of getting them to abandon that which they knew was right. So it didn't matter how pious they were; they were now on a new holy mission to depose the power-hungry Moshe. And sometimes the truth is even worth dying for. The problem was that they had accepted falsehood as truth.

This concept is very applicable to us as we too are human, and we too must be ever aware of the danger of ideologies that justify that which is evil and self-destructive. The difficulty is that when we are caught up in them, we don't recognize them for what they are. A person's convictions can drive him to greatness or bring him to the abyss — the only distinction being whether or not those convictions are correct.

HaShem wants us to succeed, and in every generation He provides Torah leaders to guide us. The only way that a person can know whether his ideologies are right is by consulting with the accepted Torah leaders of his time. When a person puts away his agenda and his bias and asks guidance on the Torah approach, HaShem directs him to the truth.

By Rabbi Ben Tzion Shafier

WHY HEAD COVERING? THERE ARE MANY OTHER MITZVOT WHICH ARE AS IMPORTANT

It is interesting that every Rabbi will give you answers to any question on any subject and will give you quotes from the Gemara and any other ethic book on the subject. However, on the subject of a wig we must believe that it is okay to wear a wig without any explanation which makes any sense.

When telling a women who wears a wig that it looks like real hair they often say: who said that my wig cannot look like my real hair?

Can you imagine our foremothers wearing a wig? Any kind of a wig?

Western society has come to idealize the concept of romance. Television, movies, and even advertisements teach us that there is nothing greater than the illusion of romance, and judging by the number of web sites, personal ads and dating services, it seems that there is almost an unlimited number of people looking for romance.

Yet, this same fact reveals that while many are looking, very few are finding. One needs to ask if their vision is focused in the right direction.
In Parashat Chayei Sarah, Rivka and Yitzchak find in each other, their soul mate. Thus, their courtship greatly differs from the typical courtship of the Western world.

Rabbi Dov Abraham Ben-Shorr writes;
"Yitzchak went out to supplicate (pray) in the field toward evening, and he lifted his eyes and saw, and behold! Camels were approaching" (Genesis 24:63). At that same instant, Rivka "raised her eyes and saw Yitzchak….She took her veil and covered herself".

Interestingly, when Rivka sees her future mate praying to Hashem, she recognizes him as her husband (to-be), and veils herself. Yet, this seems contrary to conventional wisdom. Didn't he need to see if he was attracted to her? Even Jewish Law requires that the groom should see his bride before the wedding to insure that he is attracted to her. So why would she veil herself? The answer is that she wanted her future husband to truly see her.

One of life's most interesting paradoxes is that the more that is revealed, the more naked one is, the more one's true essence is yet concealed.

The Torah teaches us that Yitzchak and Rivka both "lifted their eyes and saw." This is not simply a poetic phrase. The phrase, found only 50 times in the entire Torah, seems to imply a glimpse into the infinite, suggesting a vision of God, or, more precisely, a glimpse of His vision.

Each time someone "raises their eyes and sees" in the Book of Genesis, they each see a true vision of their own destiny, and it is often a vision that will govern Israel's future. It is a vision unclouded by physical trappings and preconceived ideas of what "should be."

Yitzchak and Rivka looked into each other's eyes and saw God, and the plan that awaited them. By veiling herself, she helped Yitzchak see her true essence, so that he would recognize that she was worthy of being brought into his mother's tent and becoming the next link in the building of God's chosen nation.

She hid the beauty that fades, to allow him to see the light of her soul. Once that happened, there was a place for true love to grow, as the verse continues, "…and she became his wife, and he loved her."

ברוך אתה השם אלוקינו מלך העולם עוטר ישראל בתפארה

Blessed are You, HaShem, our GOD, King of the universe, who crowns Israel with splendor!!!

It is with all my heart and soul that I thank HaShem for helping me to complete this booklet.

It was always with Divine Providence that I met the right people and found the right quotes from articles and books in which to add to my book and with Hashgacha Pratit I was able to complete this important work.

This book is not about my personal thoughts, they are the thoughts and messages of our sages.

Rabbis from whom I read their thoughts on the subject of Head Covering and Modesty.

I am presenting this booklet to you with a prayer to HaShem for all my readers to gain a deeper understanding of this mighty mitzvah of head covering, may you merit to fulfill it.

From deep inside my heart and soul I thank HaShem for the opportunity of helping me to put all those thoughts together in a booklet and bring them to you the readers.

I am grateful to HaShem for allowing me to have come in contact with loving friends who took a personal interest in this project by giving me of their time and knowledge.

The subject of head covering is very close to my heart as I personally struggled with the idea of covering my head.

Today, I feel that it is the greatest gift in which HaShem has blessed me.

The gift of having HaShem above me at all times, looking and guiding me.

My advice to women is do not miss the momentum of covering your heads.

While you have all your body parts take advantage of our short stay here on this earth and put on the crown befitting the daughter of HaShem.

You will certainly give HaShem much nachat and in return HaShem will be above you protecting you and looking over you and your family at all times.

Hashem created many diamonds and the modest women is one of those diamonds. May we all strive to be one of Hashem's diamonds.

SHALOM

For comments or more information: Contact Shoshana Harbor at:
Shoshanaharbor@gmail.com

Or call me at 937-422-2935

Made in the USA
Columbia, SC
17 July 2021